First Published 2010

Derek Good
Auckland
New Zealand

Table of Contents

How to use this book 7

Chapter One - Introduction 10

Chapter Two - What is ROI? 15

Chapter Three - Tests and Measures 25

Chapter Four - Hard and Soft Measures 34

    Isolation of measures 38

Chapter Five – The Right Language 41

Chapter Six – So What? 44

Chapter Seven - The Magic Formula 48

    Retention 54

    Productivity 58

    Morale 61

    Measuring ROI on Sales 67

Chapter Eight - RPMs Methodology 72

    Phase One 74

    Predicting ROI 78

    Phase Two 82

    Phase Three 85

    Phase Four 88

Chapter Nine - Applications and Examples 90

    HR Initiatives & Training 90

    Marketing 92

    Capital Expenditure 93

    Recruitment 94

Chapter Ten - When to Say No 97

Chapter Eleven – Accountability, Mankind's Vanishing Virtue 99

Chapter Twelve - Ten Tips for getting a business case signed off 103

    Answers to exercises 105

    Recommended Reading List 106

    Testimonials from ROI workshop attendees 107

    Derek Good Bio 108

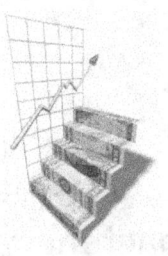

Foreword

The world has frequently experienced periods of economic uncertainty. In fact, it seems more likely that market economies can alter very quickly as the years pass. A wobble in the markets in Europe send shock waves across the Atlantic. Even events in remote parts of the world seem to trigger impact on larger economies. While economies are somewhat fragile, trying to get investment in some areas – in particular training and HR programmes is somewhat difficult. What is it that prevents organisations from investing in the times when their people need it most? If there is ever a need for people to be at their best or a call for more loyalty from its people, it's when there are shortages.

When economies stabilise and there is more movement in the labour market, organisations that provided investment in employees are more likely to see them want to support their organisations and managers further. So, although companies tighten their investment belts during troubled times, they may suffer when things return to stability.

The main reason organisations (or the decision makers in those organisations) don't invest in HR and training programmes is because they fail to link the outcomes to tangible benefits. Some people see training as a 'nice to have' but not essential which often means they haven't thought it through. As an example, if you employed someone to operate a new piece of machinery, you wouldn't dream of letting them figure it out for themselves. You would expect them to be trained on how to utilise it properly ensuring they knew the safety aspects and how to operate it at best performance. Why? Well presumably because you have invested in the machinery and don't want it damaged. Oh and probably because you won't want a lawsuit or any bad press about injuries caused by your negligence. A further consideration may be that you want to maximise the output of the machine so you want them to know how to operate it at optimum performance levels. Okay - that all makes sense but how does that apply to training someone who doesn't operate machinery – like a receptionist for example?

Well, here's the key point. For the same reasons you wouldn't let someone loose on an expensive piece of machinery, you really shouldn't let them loose on your most important assets – your customers. They can do as much damage to your bottom line without training on how to deal with your customers optimally as they can without being trained on how to run your precious piece of kit.

Think about the statistics you have probably heard in the past. One negative experience will mean the customer will tell 9, 12, 15 people? Whatever the number – it's probably high. The people they tell may or may not act on it – but chances are it will affect their choices and they may tell others and so on. It's therefore critical to understand what our customers are worth. Knowing that Mr or Mrs Customer is going to come back time and again is worth knowing. If you're working in a supermarket and the customer has $150 worth of groceries in their shopping trolley – your interaction with them is not just worth the $150 – it's $150 multiplied by the number of times they do a big shop there. If that's monthly and they'll live there for ten years, your $150 shop is suddenly $18,000! Now as the owner of the store, you may comprehend that – but as the shelf stacker – do you care?

One positive, helpful experience provided by employees 'trained' on how to engage customers can win people over for a long time. Conversely, one idle, sarcastic comment can destroy any hope of repeat business from a disgruntled customer.

So, training to create motivated, skilful and knowledgeable employees can really save money, improve profits and provide a return for what you spend in helping get that way.

How do you do it? How do you help your manager see it that way and how do you get that business case signed off? Well, read on and discover the most basic and simplistic explanation of ROI in the world today. Forget about expensive calculations, weeks of effort gathering data and lengthy formulas that take days to work out. If you can get the result in principle worked out in minutes, you can convince the ever busy manager of the merits of your plan. This book will provide you with key insights, simple formulas and practical thinking to help you understand ROI like never before and arm you for the boardroom with a solid business case.

What you read in this book is a guide at looking at the business impact and monetary consequence of just about any investment. As you read this book, we guarantee you will find ways to apply the principles in your business immediately.

We have simplified the topic of ROI and will help you write a convincing business case by showing tangible benefits.

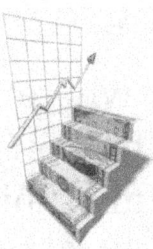

How to use this book

This is a practical book. One of the best ways to retain information is to apply it quickly. So, during this book you will see a number of symbols. These will help you know what to do next. One of the biggest problems people face is to have a knowledge overload or under load. This can be expressed as knowledge obesity & knowledge bulimia. If you have a lot of knowledge, it really does you little good unless you apply it. Likewise, reading something and not taking it in is as pointless as not applying the knowledge.

Legend to the symbols:

Example. This symbol represents an example that has been given to highlight a particular point in this book.

STOP! This is where you get to complete an exercise based on the scenario you have been given. These exercises will be used throughout the book to assist you to become familiar with the calculations.

 **Reflection.** This is where you have an opportunity to reflect on past situations and apply the principles of this book. The aim of this activity is for you to use existing knowledge and apply it to the new ideas and information you gain from studying this book.

You will find it extremely useful to have the following items with you when you study this book:

- A pad for working out figures
- A pencil
- A calculator

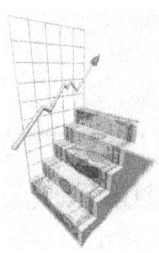

Chapter One - Introduction

In our personal lives, we have all shopped and purchased something. Think of something you bought **this week**. It may have been a cinema ticket, food, a new stereo, fuel or one of a multitude of things on offer. It may even have been a service of some kind such as dry cleaning, baby sitting or a haircut. Now, as you are thinking of that item you bought or that service you purchased, ask yourself the question, 'Did I need that?" If you answered "No" then it was likely to have been something for someone else or a "Feel Good' or "Impulse" purchase or it was something you "Wanted" rather than "Needed".

If your answer was "Yes" and you actually needed whatever it was that you exchanged money for, congratulations! Either way, make a list of what benefits you have already got from the purchase or that you expect to get from the purchase. These benefits can be as broad as you like but they must be something clearly identifiable.

Purchase:

_____

Benefits:

_____

_____

_____

Let's take the example of a cinema ticket. Okay, so you probably didn't actually need to get it, you could have done something else with your time and money but let's say it was a film you really wanted to see. Some of the benefits you will expect to receive from seeing the film may be:

- More Enlightenment – You have more knowledge now than before

- Entertainment – You were entertained while watching the movie and got a real buzz from being entertained

- Relaxation – You are now more able to cope with your duties (This incidentally may save you taking a sick day at work tomorrow for example – more on this later)

- Information to share on a current movie in a number of conversations at the bar, at work or wherever, so you can feel involved and accepted

- Upliftment – Knowledge that life is not so bad which also helps you to cope with things as they are
- Relationship – spending time together with a partner, friend, relative

This is not an exhaustive list, although it does provide some good justification for spending some money and receiving the benefits. The outcome of these things is the Return on the Investment you have made for purchasing the cinema ticket. The returns listed above can be described as measures, as they are quantifiable outcomes from the experience. Measures are discussed further in chapter three. Although these measures are somewhat intangible in this example, I will show you how to develop them into more tangible measures later on.

In your everyday life, you probably don't consider too much the measures of purchasing a cinema ticket because the investment is relatively small. Many of us will have come out of the cinema at some point in our lives stating that the movie we had just seen was terrible – which of course would have been a bad investment, not just of our money but also of our time.

Time is one commodity we should be careful about what it's invested in. Money we can always get more of but time is always a finite resource. A successful businessman once said

'You can always get or make more money but you cannot get more time, invest it wisely'.

I have found most people to be extremely careful when they spend a lot of money on something such as a new car, house or a holiday. You may even have made a list like the one earlier for a purchase of this kind without really realising that you were predicting your Return on Investment. I am sure though, that you made sure you had some idea of the potential benefits you were going to receive from parting with that money or from making such a financial commitment.

You may be familiar with the saying, "When my ship comes in". This saying has been used to refer to the time in the future when someone gets a break, a success or a windfall of money comes their way. Well, the reference of this saying dates back a few centuries when wealthy European merchants awaited their ships returning from the Orient laden with spices, silk and other treasures from the East. This then they would sell for great profit and was a time greatly looked forward to by the owners. However, that is only half the story. You see, to expect to have your ship come in, you first had to send one out and not just an empty ship, you had to send it out stocked with goods from your homeland in order to sell in the Orient so you could buy more items to bring home. The added benefit then being that you would make a double profit. The point of the story then is that these merchants invested heavily at the outset, then received a very positive return on that investment.

So, personally, we are okay with parting with our personal money so long as we get something in return. In basic terms, every week we exchange some form of currency, usually money, for a product or service from somebody else. How do we feel about that in business?

Chapter Two - What is ROI?

ROI or Return on Investment is what is measured in return for an outlay. Normally, we refer to this in monetary terms, although it could easily be done for Time. For example, we may be tempted to take a short cut while walking because it will give us more time at the other end and may even save some energy; a worthy investment of taking the short cut.

There will always be a return on any investment; it's just not always necessarily going to be a positive return each time. Negative return on investment or 'When to walk away' will be covered in chapter ten, though for now, it is sufficient to mention that working out or predicting your ROI will help you determine a good or a bad investment.

In simple terms ROI is the measure of how the benefits of an investment stack up against the actual investment. You can work out these benefits in any way you wish. There may be a host of measures that come out and these can be placed in two categories: Hard measures and Soft measures. These will be covered in more detail in Chapter Four although you probably have a good idea about the difference between the two. Hard measures are those which are quite tangible such as retention of staff members, while soft measures are things such as improved team work or higher morale.

You will do well to remember that hard measures are those that will provide a more definable return on the investment which will enable those with the purse strings to pay more attention to the proposal.

Firstly, the net gain of an investment is measured like this:

In an example of winning at the casino, if you win $10,000 GREAT! But if you have spent $6,000 to win the $10,000 then your NET gain is actually only $4,000!

So, the actual gain is only that which is left after the initial cost is removed.

The return on investment is expressed as a percentage. Much the same as when someone receives a pay rise, the percentage increase is shown as the increase after the original amount has been deducted.

As an example, someone earning $50,000 and receives an additional $10,000 as a pay rise, their net gain is $10,000 i.e. $60,000 (The new amount in total) - $50,000 (The original amount). Expressed as a percentage, this then is:

$60,000 - $50,000 divided by $50,000 x 100% = 20%

The above formula is a simple mathematical and business equation for working out increases or decreases in amounts relative to a starting figure. It is exactly the same in working out ROI.

The formula is expressed as:

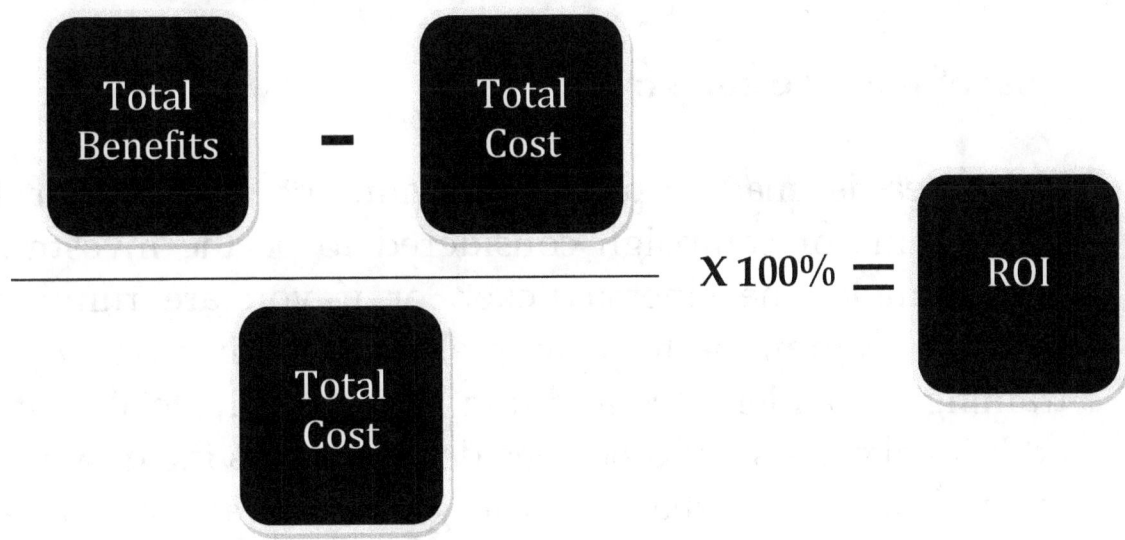

So, what does this formula actually mean? Let's take it stage by stage:

Benefits of the investment:

As described in Chapter One, the benefits of the investment should be everything gained from the investment itself. As in our example in the first chapter, these included six areas for purchasing the cinema ticket. You will notice that a number of these areas could be considered soft measures or those without a necessary monetary value attached. In working out a positive return on investment, all possible benefits should be listed. The most important of these in getting sign off for the investment will be the hard measures, or those that can be attributed to a direct monetary value.

Cost of the investment:

This area is made up of the value of the cost of the programme or campaign considered to be the investment. For example, the cinema ticket, or if you are running a training programme for example, the costs incurred by the training provider. In addition to the financial outlay, additional costs should be considered such as the down time for staff to attend, the cost in organisation and any loss of sales due to the time spent on the programme.

Think about all the hidden costs that you may not normally include when you are making an investment:

_____

_____

_____

_____

_____

_____

Here are some of our examples:

- Staff away from their roles
- Replacement staff on the phones
- Loss of sales
- Interrupted service to customers

Rest of the formula:

The top line of the formula, Benefits minus the cost, provides the monetary gain or loss of the investment. However, to work out the percentage Return on investment, the formula requires the net benefit (ie – Benefits minus the cost) to be divided by the cost and multiplied by 100% - much the same as working out the profitability factor.

 Let's take a training programme for 20 people. Let's say the training programme is aimed at increasing sales and that it costs $5,000 to run the programme.

Due to measurements, it is identified that an annual turnover increase of $100,000 is gained from the programme. With a profitability of 30%, this means that a net increase of $30,000 is gained net for the organisation:

$$\$100,000 \times 30\% = \$30,000$$

We put these figures in to the formula but first, we total up the additional costs. In this case, let's say the down time for the employees and the loss of sales for the training for a day amounted to $7,000, the formula would then be shown as:

Total Benefits of the programme : $30,000

Total Costs of investment: $5,000 + $7,000 = $12,000

$$\frac{\text{Total Benefits} - \text{Total Cost}}{\text{Total Cost}} \times 100\% = \text{ROI}$$

Or our example here:

$$\frac{\$30,000 - \$12,000}{\$12,000} \times 100\% = 150\%$$

So, the ROI of the programme for the first year is 150% or $18,000.

How complex should an ROI calculation be? Well, there will be many who will tell you that unless you have some complicated formula, a degree in mathematics and thick glasses enabling you to look at all kinds of contributing factors each having a minute effect on the overall outcome, you won't be able to measure an ROI. The perception of the complexity of these models and studies is enough to put off most people from even attempting to work out a successful model. In the end, a cost benefit analysis is the basic form of the ROI model and the simpler the better.

What are you trying to achieve by working out the ROI model?

Presumably, you are trying to see if a particular investment will pay off for you. If that is the case, you want a clear, straight forward mechanism to check out the figures. More often than not, a simple formula will provide you with a clear understanding of high benefits or low benefits. If it is a close call, you may be forced to make a judgement call or go into further detail. Generally however, you will find clear outcomes defined from a basic model which will save time and provide clarity to others in your organisation.

The total return on any investment can also be taken in short and long term measures. For example, if you are looking to predict the ROI of a marketing programme to sell a number of widgets, you may start by seeing how much revenue you generate from the advert by totalling the sales within a defined timeframe – this is the short term measure. However, how many of these purchasers will be new customers? And what is the lifetime value of a customer? The long term measure.

It is possible to have the short term return become the justification for the investment and the long term return a complete bonus. When attempting to get sign off for a business case, list absolutely everything which could be considered a financial benefit as well as anything that can relate to a current business objective.

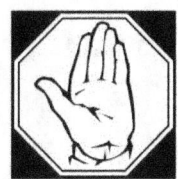

The following is an example for you to work through in order to help solidify this principle and equation:

Exercise 1. You have a small team of 10 people. You identify that over the year, you can increase their sales ability through an incentive scheme. The scheme will cost you $12,000 to run throughout the year including all additional costs. As a result, you manage to bring in $240,000 of additional business, directly attributable to the incentive scheme. Calculate the ROI on the programme if your profitability is 10%. (Answers at the back of the book).

_____

_____

_____

_____

_____

Chapter Three - Tests and Measures

In the world around us, we seem to measure everything. When you shop for vegetables, you pay on either the number of vegetables or their weight. Sporting events show measures against time or previous records of some kind. We get paid according to our measure of time. Like it or not, we exist to be constantly measured!

So what's wrong with that? Well, nothing as long as something gets done with the measurement. We're happy in life as something is normally done with the measurement. When we measure the food we want to buy, we exchange money for it. When we keep score in a sporting event, we are either happy that we beat the target because we won or sad if we do not because we have lost. When we submit a time sheet or have completed a month's work, we get paid for it.

Here's an example:

Let's say someone offers you a job to work for them for $10 per hour. You would like to be aware if this is a good return for YOUR investment. Your investment is your time, your knowledge, your experience, your contacts, your expertise etc. This then must be considered before accepting the deal.

Whenever we make a purchase or investment, some form of measurement should be in place to discover whether or not the money or the time was well spent. Returning to the example in the introduction of the cinema ticket, we often make a clear measurement of the investment either during or after the film. When was the last time you made a measurement of the last piece of capital equipment you purchased?

The reason this chapter is headed "Tests and Measures' is because sometimes, we may find it difficult to predict the ROI. In these cases, we should 'test' out the investment. In advertising for example, running an advert should lead us to test the response. Perhaps we are trying to determine the best periodical to place our campaign with. Without testing the response of a small advert first at minimal expense, we may be heading down an expensive exercise. Some things just may not work.

There are six words we commonly hear that make us wonder how we ever managed to progress to this hi-tech state we are in:

"We've always done it that way!"

I cringe when I hear those words. The saying is so true, "If you always do what you've always done, you'll always get what you've always got." If you're happy with that, then fine and you might as well stop reading. However, the fact that you have read this far probably means that you're not happy with that. So let's continue.

Here's a little quiz for you……see how well you do.

1. What is your company turnover?

    Answer   _____

2. What is your company net profit percentage?

    Answer   _____

3. How many customers does your company have?

    Answer   _____

4. What is the average sale value per order for your company?

    Answer   _____

5. What is the average number of transactions a customer has with your company per year?

    Answer   _____

6. What is the lifetime value of one of your customers?

    Answer   _____

So, how did you do?

0 to 2 - Expected.
3 to 4 - You are probably privy to sensitive information
6   - Excellent!

Knowing any of this information is valuable and in some ways essential. Knowing the company turnover gives you some indication of your size. Knowing your net profit percentage tells you how many sales you need to make to actually add to the bottom line. For example, if your company net profit percentage is 10%, then you need to sell $1,000 dollars of goods or services to make the company $100 after all expenses, costs and salaries are paid.

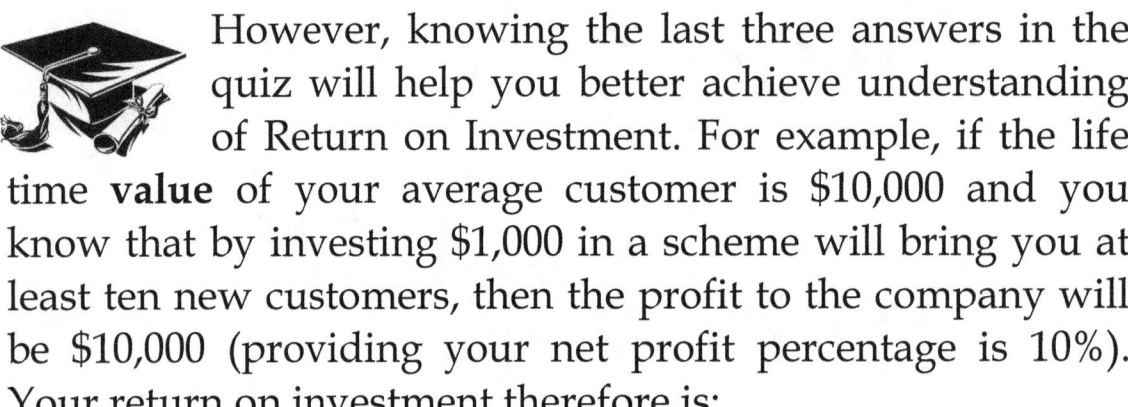 However, knowing the last three answers in the quiz will help you better achieve understanding of Return on Investment. For example, if the life time **value** of your average customer is $10,000 and you know that by investing $1,000 in a scheme will bring you at least ten new customers, then the profit to the company will be $10,000 (providing your net profit percentage is 10%). Your return on investment therefore is:

$$\frac{\$10{,}000 - \$1{,}000}{\$1{,}000} \times 100\% = \mathbf{900\%\ ROI}$$

Without the knowledge of the life time value of the customer, it would be difficult to work out the return on that investment.

When running a campaign, simply by checking the outcome or testing its results can help you identify if you are on the right track or not.

Lifetime value of a customer is extremely important when you want to use techniques to retain them. It is five times more difficult to gain a new customer than it is to retain an existing customer.

68% of customers that change suppliers do so due to perceived indifference from the current supplier – not because they have had a bad experience. Most people that have a bad experience just don't go back. In fact, most businesses only hear from about 4% of their dissatisfied customers! So if you get a complaint – be grateful someone said something to you!

In order to retain customers therefore, you may have to invest in keeping them happy and showing them you care and that you want their business. This investment in retaining customers may include such things as having a good account management system – i.e., regular contact with customers, even when they are not purchasing at the time. Some excellent customer service techniques and relationship management so that they enjoy dealing with your organisation. You may need to be doing mail outs to keep in contact. All of these things will be considered the investment in retaining customers.

In our formula, this would read as:

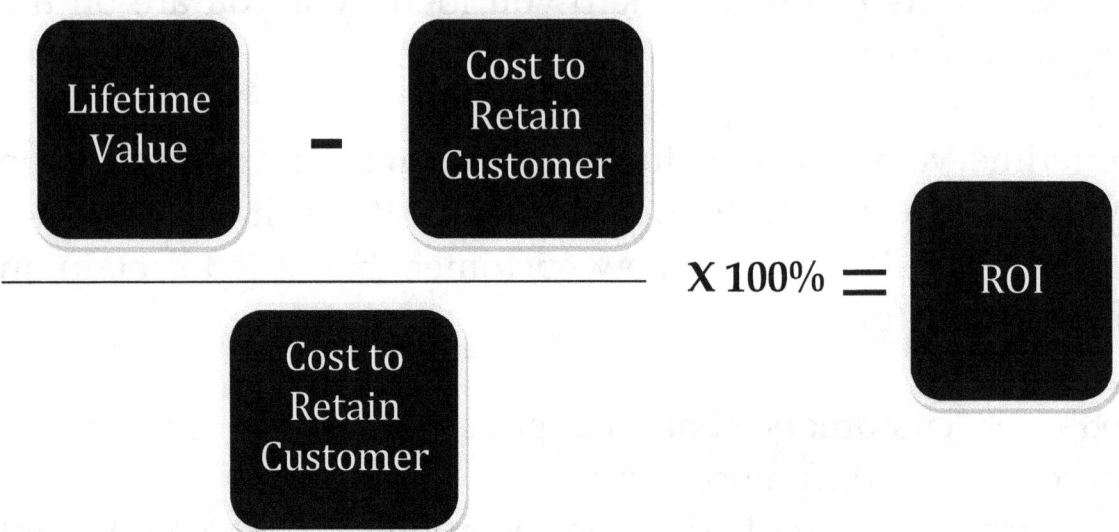

In contrast, the cost of gaining a new customer could be worked out by calculating your advertising, having sales representatives and all their expenses, branding costs etc and dividing all these costs by the number of new customers you receive each year. It will be highly likely that these costs will far outweigh those employed to retain customers.

The following is an example for you to work through in order to help solidify this principle and equation:

Exercise 2. Let's say your average value (in profit) of a particular customer is $5,000 and it costs you $2,000 to keep them through a rewards scheme, letters etc. What is your ROI for doing those additional things? (Answers at the back of the book).

_____

_____

_____

Chapter Four - Hard and Soft Measures

When talking about some investments such as training or attending seminars, people often refer to the benefits of the training as things such as:

- "It will be good for the people"
- "We will see improved teamwork"
- "Morale will increase"

Although these are all pretty good reasons to go ahead, they may actually not be measurable. In these cases, they are considered to be 'Soft' measures. In contrast, the following may be measured quite accurately:

- Increased Productivity
- Increased Sales
- Retention of customers

As the above areas are clearly definable, they are considered to be 'Hard' measures as the impact of the investment may be measured against a 'Before and After' scenario.

As an example, a company employee normally takes 30 minutes to perform a task, such as a loan approval. Over the year, this worker completes 400 loan approvals. Due to a change in process or training, this task now only takes 15 minutes to complete. From that, we can begin to measure the impact in monetary terms as follows:

If the worker is paid at $20 per hour, we can offer the following calculation:

400 tasks x ¼ hours x $20 per hour = $2,000 annual saving

It's a saving in monetary terms, as this person's time may now be directed in to performing other tasks or they can now double the amount of loan approvals.

So, if the training cost the organisation $500, the ROI would be:

$$\frac{\$2,000 - \$500}{\$500} \times 100\% = 300\% \text{ ROI}$$

In the following chapter, we will discuss the 'Magic Formula' for the ROI argument. This formula will demonstrate the blending of soft and hard measures.

Some people will have a very 'left brain' attitude to investments and expenditures which means they will be analytical of any spend. These people are very often in the decision making positions such as CEOs, General Managers and accountants. It is these people especially that need to see hard measures predicted, visible or achieved in order to see 'value' in the investment. We will discuss this further in the chapter entitled, 'The Right Language'.

One of the best areas to focus on in order to provide evidence of success or failure is to start measuring outcomes. Measuring areas that you have control over will allow you to explore benefits of making changes, employing new concepts, altering initiatives and planning for growth. These concepts were covered in the previous chapter on Tests and measures.

How do we effectively measure? Well, there are some great models out there, although we should make sure we are making the measures relative. For example in D.L. Kirkpatrick's model, which has been around for a number of years and widely used as a methodology for measuring the effectiveness of programmes, the recommendation is to measure the following:
1. Reaction
2. Learning
3. Application
4. Business Impact

You need to ensure that the measures are relative TO those areas and relative IN those areas to YOUR business.

1. Reaction. You could do this in the form of feedback sheets or surveys. This seems to work well following a training programme. It is quite common to request immediate feedback in this way. However, it is also common to ask irrelevant questions such as, 'How did you rate the presenter?' or 'How was lunch?' These questions have absolutely no business impact. Whereas a question like, 'Will you apply this training today back in your workplace?' tells us if we hit the mark or not, or a question like, 'How relevant were these principles to your role today?' will help ascertain whether or not people gained anything from the training.

2. Learning. This can be done with some form of test. Learning is different from application. We need to determine whether they have taken on board the principles trained on.

3. Application. This is where you determine whether or not the learning is being applied – probably the most important measure. You can do this by live coaching or evaluation sessions.

4. Business Impact. After you have delivered the programme and assess that learning and application has been taking place, you can measure the impact in the business. For example, are the number of complaints down, are sales up, are more customers being served etc. This will translate in to turnover and profit increases – easy measures.

So, measuring needs to be relevant, engaged in soon after the programme has started and constant. When performance is measured, performance improves. When performance is measured and reported, the rate of improvement increases. We shall discuss reporting in the form of accountability in a later chapter.

Isolation of measures

One of the most common questions posed in looking at ROI and training interventions in particular is "How do you know that the intervention was the thing that made the difference or created the impact? This is referring to isolating the intervention or measure involved. This is often the one thing that prevents people from either putting measures in place or from bothering to look at an ROI in the first place.

In reality, it can be a lot simpler than it first looks. Let's take for example Sales Training. At the same time as the training happening, you may also have had a marketing campaign take place or some extra expenditure in advertising or branding. How then do you attribute any additional sales to just the training? Well, in this case, you need to look at a measure that captivates the training itself. In this case, it's probably something like improvement in the sales conversion rate. Extra advertising or branding may bring in more leads and extra sales purely because more leads are coming in but the sales conversion still needs to take place and the percentage rate won't go up as a result of just extra branding revenue. So, in this case, you will have a trend in conversion rate prior to the training, then look at measuring the conversion rate after the training.

Sure, sales should go up as a result of additional advertising but this in itself should increase the number of leads. The conversion rate – without any training to improve it, will also remain constant. Therefore, the measure to put in place could be 'increases in conversion rate'.

In the case of Difficult Caller training, you could look at a measure of 'escalations reduced'. In this instance, skills to handle difficult callers could be the intervention. How do you know if it's been successful? Well, you need to measure something that it will improve. In one instance with a finance company, the manager received around two escalations calls a day. These escalations each took half an hour to resolve. Following targeted training for his staff to handle the calls more effectively, this dropped to one escalation call every two weeks.

Measure what you are targeting. Look for ways to isolate the benefit of the intervention. Also, ensure that the steps of measurement are in place. In our last example for difficult caller training, measure the application (listening to the staff on the calls for their application of the skills) as well as the impact on the business (e.g. reduced escalations to the manager).

In all areas, the best way to isolate is to have a control group. Do something different with one group that you aren't doing with all the others. If marketing and HR are all doing something for the company as well as you wanting to try out some training, take a few random people and pilot the training with them and measure the difference from the rest of the organisation.

Chapter Five – The Right Language

In any visit to a foreign land, it pays to know a little bit about the local customs and the language. You can tend to get by on a small amount of phrases and key words in order to be comfortable, understand people and most importantly for others to be able to know where you're coming from. There's nothing worse than not being able to communicate and having both parties become frustrated.

Think back at the last time you had a conversation with someone where either you or the other party were struggling to comprehend one another. It may not have even been a compatibility issue with language, it may indeed have been a problem with the way one of you were putting across your point of view.

Ensuring people understand our position is also a problem not limited with language. People will describe the same experience in different ways. A hundred people will see the same movie and have different opinions of the plot, the characters, the moral of the story and even the actor's ability. Eating a meal in a restaurant will often leave diners with a different view on the quality of food, the service of the staff and the value of the meal. It all depends on our points of view, the mood we are in, the experience of how it all relates to us and so forth. We are all different and we all have different priorities, likes and dislikes.

One of the most important things to consider in putting together a business case is to ensure it is written in 'the language' of the person who is going to sign-off. This means that although you may see great merit in the benefits of the proposal, they may translate into something little more than a 'nicety' to the person you are presenting the case to.

One of the reasons for the failure of success in business case approach is because the person giving sign off is normally someone who is very analytical or 'left brain' focussed. The brain is divided in two halves, the right side deals very much with our creative side, the left side with figures and logic. It's easy to remember which is which by the letters themselves. 'L' for left hand of the brain is hard and straight – logic. 'R' is curvy, signifying a more artistic or creative streak. Here are some of the differences between left brain and right brain indicators:

Left Brian	**Right Brain**
Analytical	Big Picture
Detail Focussed	Creative
Bottom Line	Impulsive
Less Emotional	More Emotional

In explaining this, we can see that a 'left brain' focus on figures, results, bottom line profit etc. will be looking for those exact things in any business case. Even though there may be great benefit illustrated in some of the 'soft' areas given in the business case, these will not necessarily translate in to turnover, profit or impact on the business. So, we need to blend in those soft and hard measures or put them in to the language of the person who will be signing off the proposal. One way of helping to get this way of thinking cemented is to drill down to the real reason for the business case or proposal. We will discuss this in the next chapter entitled, 'So What?'

Chapter Six – So What?

You may be wondering what a heading such as this is doing in this book. Well, we think it is one of the most important questions you can ever ask yourself. It will help provide a solid foundation for whatever you are doing, or it will help you to decide to forget about it. Either way, it's an invaluable concept to buy into.

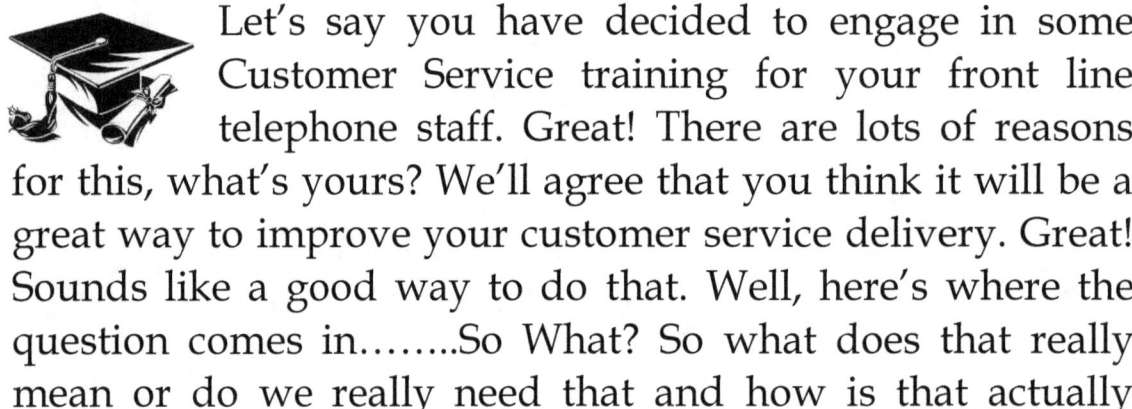

Let's say you have decided to engage in some Customer Service training for your front line telephone staff. Great! There are lots of reasons for this, what's yours? We'll agree that you think it will be a great way to improve your customer service delivery. Great! Sounds like a good way to do that. Well, here's where the question comes in……..So What? So what does that really mean or do we really need that and how is that actually going to help?

Let's take this scenario a little deeper. You want to train on customer service skills to improve your customer service delivery…SO WHAT? So the customers will have a better experience in dealing with our organisation…SO WHAT? So they will want to come back to us again…SO WHAT? So we will increase the amount of transactions they make with us…SO WHAT? So our turnover will increase…SO WHAT? So we will make more profit.

Ah hah!!!

so what you're saying is, you want to engage in some customer service training to help improve the profits of the organisation? Well that sounds like a great idea – a real impact on the business.

What we've done here is to dig much deeper into the real benefit or reason for doing what we started with. When we analyse it, we see that this actually is a great way to do something for the business. In addition to building the confidence and skills of the front line telephone staff and helping our customers experience a better level of service, we will see an increase in profits.

Let's detail this scenario:

1. We want Customer Service Training which means:
2. Better customer experience which means:
3. Happier customers which means:
4. Increased custom from our existing customers which means
5. Higher turnover which means
6. Higher profits

In addition to these benefits, there will likely be an increased number of referrals coming in and possibly an alignment to one of the organisation's business objectives which is probably something along the lines of 'Improving Service Delivery.'

 Now think of something you asked for recently in a business situation. It may have been some stationery, an advertising solution, a new computer, a raise in salary, an afternoon off etc. Whatever it was, ask yourself the question, 'So What?' Then ask it again and again until you can drill it right down to an impact on the business that can be measurable and positive.

Try this out next time you have a need to ask for something else. It's a great question to ask. If you are a manager, try asking your team members the same question. It really gets you thinking and helps to rationalise or throw out requests that have no impact eventually on the business.

Try this exercise on 'So What?'

Write one thing you wanted recently then try the 'So What?' test:

1.

2.

3.

4.

5.

6.

7.

What is your AH HAH?

Chapter Seven - The Magic Formula

One of the keys in getting sign off for a business case that may seem difficult to get, even though you know the benefits for the company will be amazing but you just can't prove it is to put the benefits in language those holding the purse strings will understand. This language is…..money (bottom line).

Some previously thought "soft" measures can be translated into "hard" measures by applying the formula shown in this chapter.

Looking at most of the concerns in a "people" environment, we discovered that the people element of any organisation presents some of the greatest challenges. Conversely, having the right people highly motivated in their roles can bring about incredible results for the same organisation. Indeed, the right people are a company's greatest asset and managers need to ensure they are doing all they can to create the environment in which their people are keen to come back to work everyday.

Jim Goodnight who owns one of the world's largest privately owned software company, SAS, in America, was interviewed on his amazing techniques for keeping staff. His employee turnover is way below the industry average in the software business and in an interview he stated "95% of my assets drive out of the gate every night, it's my job to ensure they come back tomorrow".

SAS has such a revolutionary way of treating its staff that its business methods are now taught at Harvard. With over 40,000 customer sites worldwide and over 10,000 employees he is doing something right. He saw the value of his employees and is making continuous investments to keep them happy.

Some of the problem areas with people are listed here:

- Attendance
- Punctuality
- Job Satisfaction
- Retention
- Customer satisfaction
- Performance management
- Stress
- Recognition
- Attitude
- Ability
- Productivity

- Career development
- Job skills
- Confidence
- Being valued
- Professional standards
- Time management
- Morale & Motivation
- Understanding of procedures & systems
- Personal responsibility

And the list could go on and on.

We also discovered that they can be slotted in to three segments. A fourth was added a little later in order to provide extra "Zest" to the formula without taking anything away. These segments are:

Retention

Productivity

Morale

Sales

As seems to be commonplace in today's "Let's make everything quicker" world, the four segments produce an acronym 'RPMS' which is the basis for the RPMs Methodology – explained in the next chapter. RPMs which simulate the rev counter for a vehicle is 'revolutions per minute' is a measure used to determine how hard a car engine is working.

Most people in their adult lives will experience driving a motor vehicle. In doing so, they will have been in control of one of the great inventions known as the combustion engine. This reference to RPMs has significance to a motor vehicle.

Most cars currently use a four-stroke combustion cycle to convert gasoline into motion. The four-stroke approach was invented in 1867 by Nikolaus Otto. The four strokes are:

1. Intake stroke
2. Compression stroke
3. Combustion stroke
4. Exhaust stroke

"The easiest way to remember this is suck, squeeze, bang, blow!"

The piston is connected to the crank shaft by a connecting rod. As the engine goes through this cycle, the following takes place:

1. The piston starts at the top, the intake valve opens, and the piston moves down to let the engine take in a

cylinder-full of air and gasoline. This is the intake stroke. Only the tiniest drop of gasoline needs to be mixed into the air for this to work.

2. Then the piston moves back up to compress this fuel/air mixture. Compression makes the explosion more powerful.

3. When the piston reaches the top of its stroke, the spark plug emits a spark to ignite the gasoline. The gasoline charge in the cylinder explodes, driving the piston down.

4. Once the piston hits the bottom of its stroke, the exhaust valve opens and the exhaust leaves the cylinder to go out the tail pipe.

Now the engine is ready for the next cycle, so it intakes another charge of air and gas.

In an engine the linear motion is converted into rotational motion by the crank shaft. The rotational motion is used to turn (rotate) the car's wheels.

So, that's the engine. The RPM, or Revolutions per minute, is how many times the four processes are completed in a minute. Like most of us, this is easily gauged by the 'REV' counter on the dash board. This counter normally has single digits on it which are to be multiplied by 1,000. You will have noticed a section coloured in red towards the far right of the dial to indicate 'over revving' the engine or putting it under severe stress. Also, on the far left, in the lower rev count area, the car is unlikely to make much of an impact on the road as the engine is considered to be idling. The key to successful and long lasting car care is to keep the rev counter between its idle state and the danger red area.

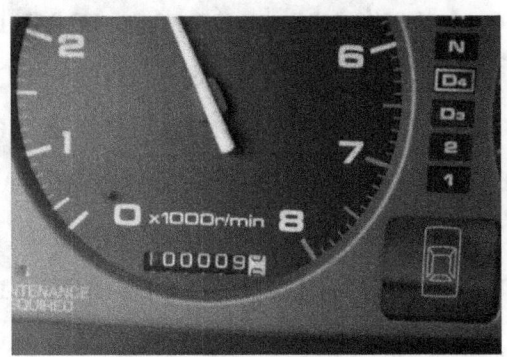

Similarly, your organisation or centre also needs to be running above idle mode and out of the high stress area to ensure a smooth operation and a healthy functionality, hence the likeness for our formula of RPMs.

So, getting back to that enormous list of people problem areas in your organisation, certain aspects of these potential problem areas could fit under more than one of these headings – Retention, Productivity and Morale. For example, time management. As a staff member becomes more efficient in managing their daily tasks through an improved ability to manage their time, at least two things will happen: firstly, they will show an increase in productivity and secondly, they will have an increase in morale because they are accomplishing more. Likewise, job satisfaction: as a person's job satisfaction increases in their role, they will find more reasons to want to be at work and have a happier well-being. This will improve their morale and the organisation's likelihood of retaining them longer.

So, an HR initiative – perhaps training, may be the form of investment sought to improve these areas and in working out the return on investment using these segments - the formula is described here. As an example, we are using a training programme or HR initiative as the investment in order to improve the performance in our key areas:

Retention:

Once you have the right people in the organisation, you want to retain them for as long as possible. Although it will be incredibly difficult to reduce the attrition rate (opposite to retention – i.e., the annual percentage of those people leaving the centre) to zero, (not that you would want zero attrition as new blood into a business helps with stimulation, growth and new ideas), a structured training programme involving key skill areas, coaching and benefits for the individual will help to reduce the attrition rate.

In order to illustrate this in some clear monetary values, the first part of the RPM formula is based on the retention issue and is written like this:

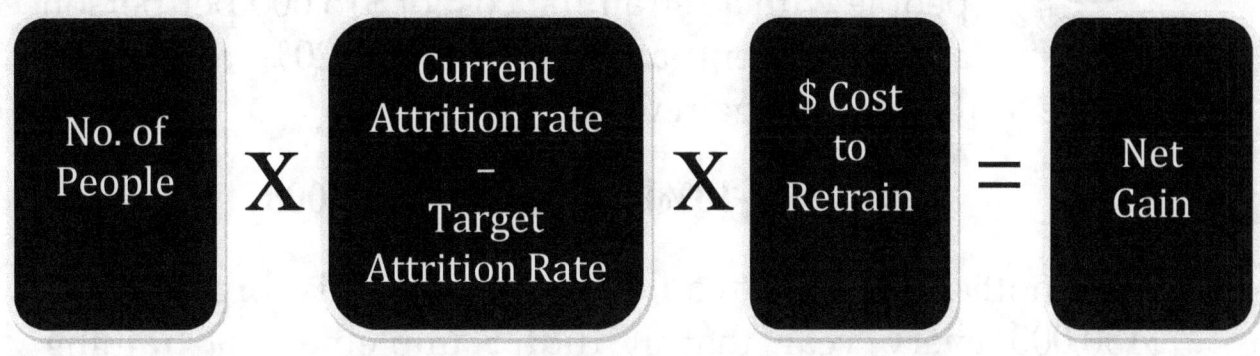

The following term definitions are described thus:

No. of people: The actual number of individuals working in the organisation

Current Attrition Rate: The current percentage annually of people leaving the centre

Target Attrition Rate: The target percentage of people leaving the business after implementing training

Cost to retrain: The actual cost of retraining a new individual. This should be composed of such things as recruitment fees, induction programme time and costs, downtime, loss of knowledge and productivity, impact on others when knowledge of departure is known etc.

ROI: The return on the investment

So, in an example of an organisation with 100 people with a retraining cost of $15,000 per person and a current attrition rate of 20% aiming to reduce to 10%, the net gain would be:

100 x (20%-10%) x $15,000 = $150,000

Put another way, it would be costing this organisation $150,000 every year that it didn't implement a training programme or some other method to improve retention. In addition to looking at staff retention, the retention of customers can also be used in this part of the formula providing justification for the retention of customers due to continued income.

Don't forget, this is the net gain. The ROI still has to go through the original formula which is:

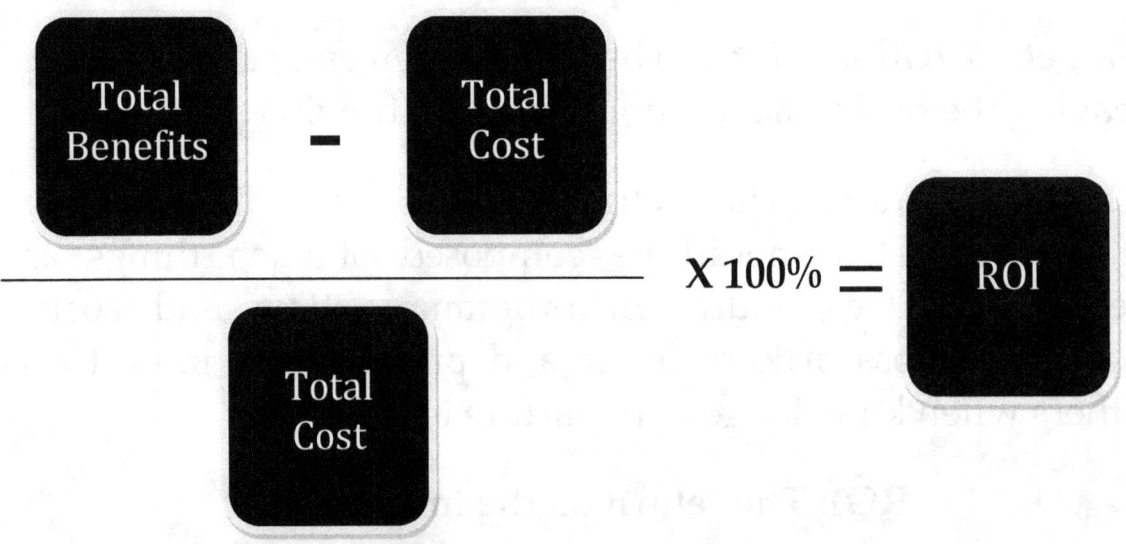

As we have no cost of the programme illustrated here, we will suggest it cost $40,000 to implement. The ROI therefore would be:

$$(\$150{,}000 - \$40{,}000) / \$40{,}000 \times 100\% = 275\% \text{ ROI}$$

The following is an example for you to work through in order to help solidify this principle and equation:

Exercise 3. Let's say you have an organisation of 50 people and the attrition rate is currently at 25%. Your retraining cost per person is rated at $25,000. Calculate the ROI on a programme that promises to reduce your attrition rate to 15% if the programme will cost in total $25,000. (Answers at the back of the book).

_____

_____

_____

_____

Productivity:

This can be measured in the amount of work a person can achieve during their working day. (It could also be used to measure an increase in sales following a successful training programme as it effectively has increased the productivity of the sales person – this would be the Sales part of the formula.)

The Productivity part of the formula is as follows:

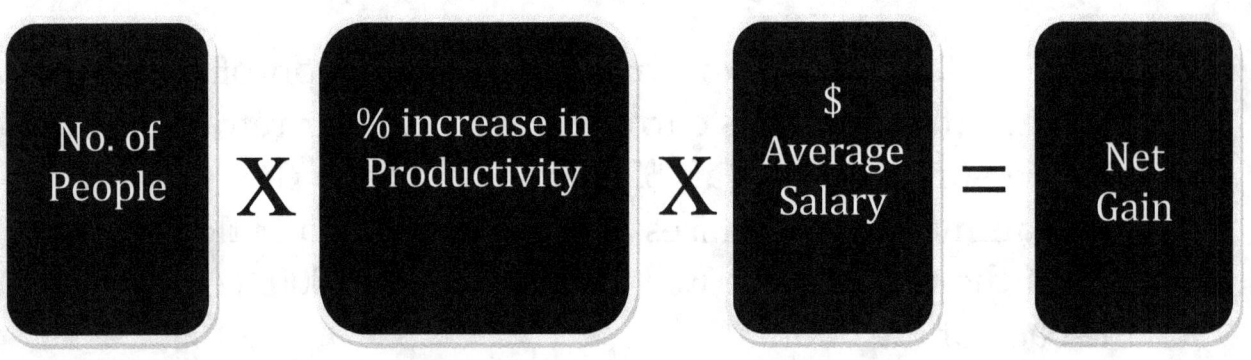

The following term definitions are described thus:

No. of people: The actual number of individuals working in the organisation

% increase in productivity: The actual amount of improved efficiency in the role of the person

Average salary: The total salary of all people in the organisation affected by the HR initiative divided by the number of people in the organisation affected by the HR initiative.

ROI: The return on the investment

Using the same example business as in the Retention part of the formula, i.e. 100 staff and taking $35,000 as the average salary and increase in productivity estimated at 5%, we would have the following:

$$100 \times 5\% \times \$35,000 = \$175,000$$

So, with the above example, with each person showing an average 5% increase in productivity through a successful training programme, the effect is the same as having five new members of staff each at a salary of $35,000. So, a 5% increase in sales could firstly represent a gain of 5 extra staff members as shown above or in monetary terms could represent an even greater ROI if the profit from additional sales revenue was greater than their salaries.

For example, an insurance company with profitability of sales of $300,000 per week increasing by 5% would show an increase of $780,000 per year!!

Don't forget, this is the net gain. The ROI still has to go through the original formula which is:

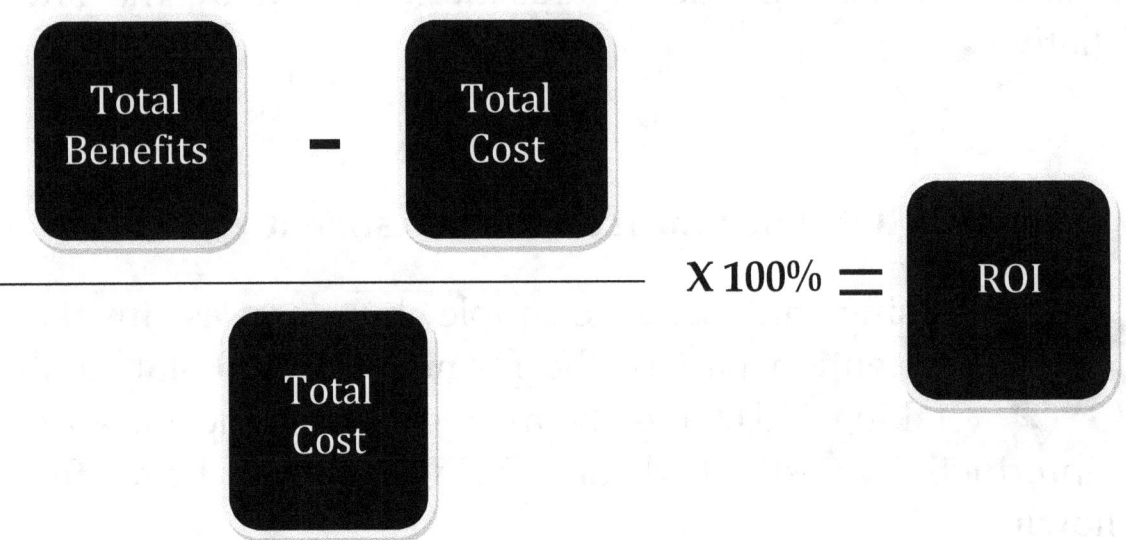

As we have no cost of the programme illustrated here, we will suggest it cost $50,000 to implement. The ROI therefore would be:

($175,000 - $50,000) / $50,000 x 100% = 250% ROI

The following is an example for you to work through in order to help solidify this principle and equation:

Exercise 4. Your organisation with 50 staff has an average salary of $45,000. With a predicted increase of 2% on average in productivity, calculate your ROI on a programme costing $15,000 to get this increase. (Answers at the back of the book).

_____

_____

_____

_____

Morale:

As stated previously, Morale is linked to both retention and productivity. In most cases the three areas are linked inexorably.

One area of having high morale is the attendance at work. People are much more likely to want to be at work when they are enthusiastic about it and are motivated by their job. This will very often transpire in to being punctual for work and coming in on those days when they don't feel 100%. In real terms, this can relate to the saving of sick days from work. When a person takes a day off work, there is a cost attributed. This cost is made up of actual paid sick leave, a temporary worker being employed, loss of productivity, loss of sales etc. Although you won't eradicate sick days altogether, you will be able to help your people avoid taking time off when they are having one of those 50/50 days.

The formula for this then is:

The following term definitions are described thus:

No. of people: The actual number of individuals working in the organisation affected by the HR initiative

Saved sick days per person per year: The realistic number of days each year for each person on average that could be saved (ie – days which ordinarily they could come to work and don't due to the fact that although they are physically able because they have low morale, they don't push themselves to come).

Cost of a sick day: This is the actual cost to an organisation for having someone off work for a day. This should include actual paid sick leave, a temporary worker being employed, loss of productivity, loss of sales, etc.

ROI: The return on the investment

 Again, if we use the same business model as in the previous two examples and work on a sick day cost of $400 and the fact that with the training programme the organisation identifies that it could save two sick days per year, then the formula would read:

$$100 \times 2 \times \$400 = \$80,000$$

Again, put another way; every year that this organisation puts off running an effective training programme to boost and raise morale; it is costing them $80,000. There are many other results from low or high morale, this is just **one** measurable.

Don't forget, this is the net gain. The ROI still has to go through the original formula which is:

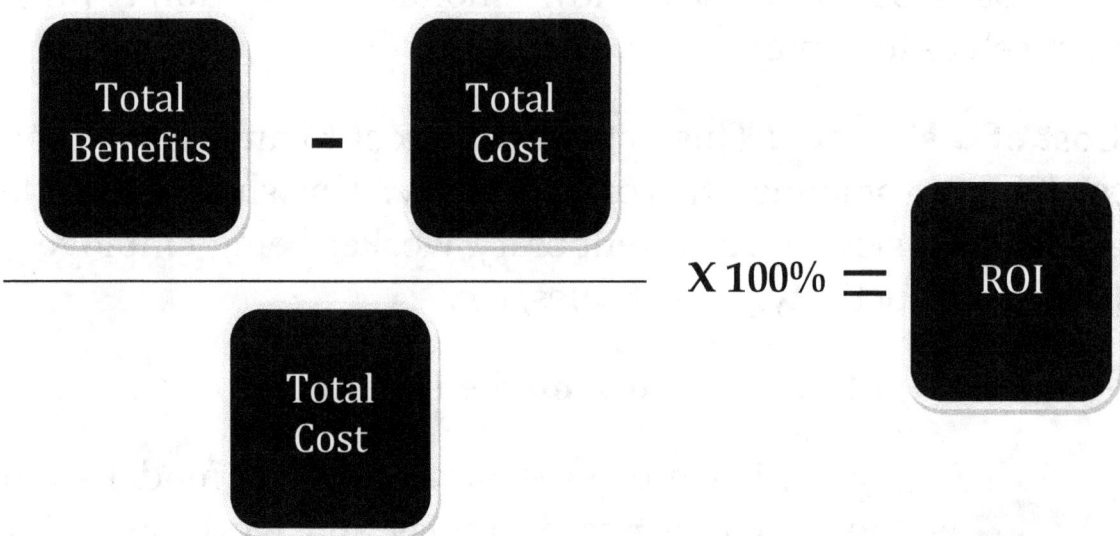

As we have no cost of the programme illustrated here, we will suggest it cost $20,000 to implement. The ROI therefore would be:

($80,000 - $20,000) / $20,000 x 100% = 300% ROI

The following is an example for you to work through in order to help solidify this principle and equation:

Exercise 5. Let's say you have an organisation of 50 people taking at least 8 sick days per person on average and the sick day cost is $800. Calculate the ROI on a programme that promises to reduce your average number of sick days by one per person if the programme will cost a total of $10,000. (Answers at the back of the book.)

_____

_____

_____

_____

When all three areas of the formula are put together, the results can be astounding:

Retention Gain + Productivity Gain + Morale Gain

=

Total Gain

In our example this equates to:

$$\$175{,}000 + \$150{,}000 + \$80{,}000 = \$405{,}000$$

If a successful training programme for 100 people costs approximately $500 per person, this would show a ROI of over 700%:

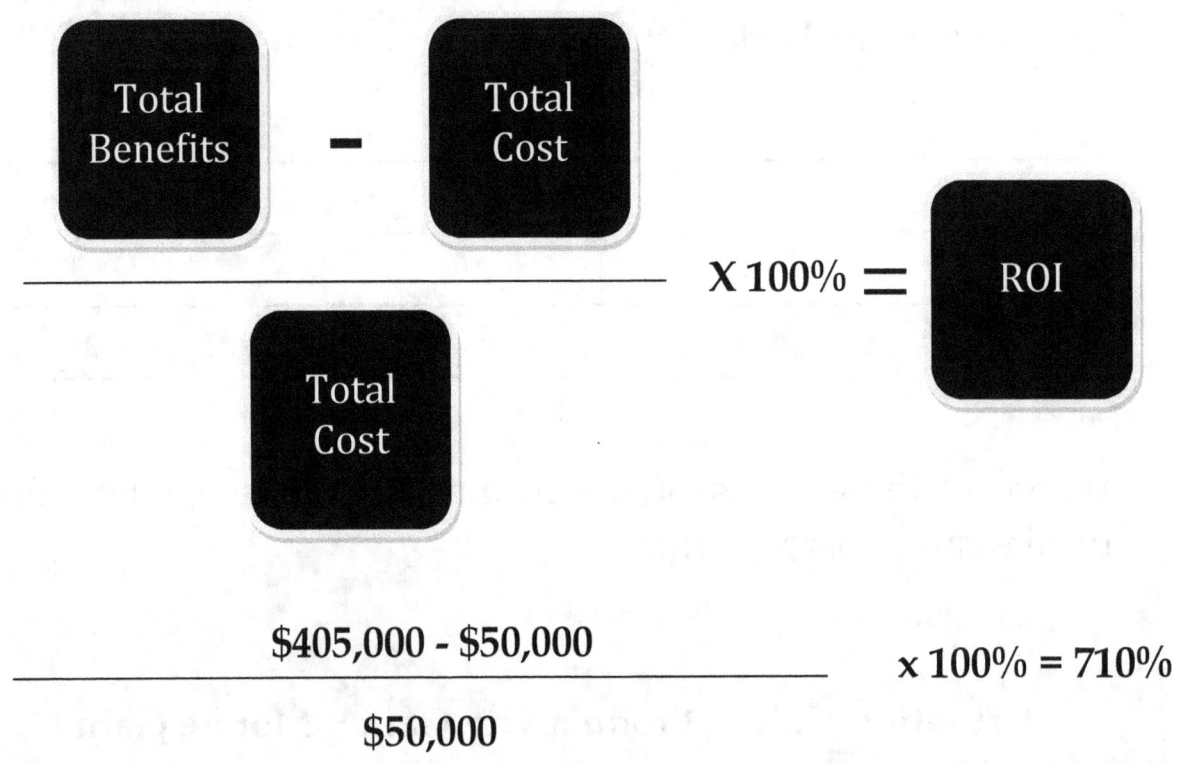

$$\frac{\$405{,}000 - \$50{,}000}{\$50{,}000} \times 100\% = 710\%$$

The above calculations show the Retention, Productivity and Morale areas of the formula. For the sales component of working out any ROI, it is effectively the same as Productivity and can be shown as:

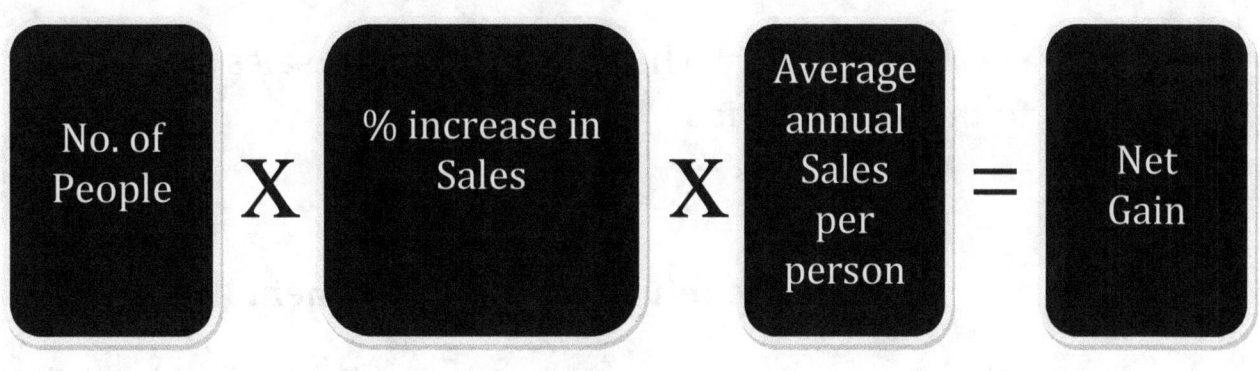

No. of people

X

% increase in sales

X

$average annual sales per person

=

Net Gain

The following term definitions are described thus:

No. of people: The actual number of individuals working in the organisation in the sales department

% increase in sales: The actual percentage increase of improved sales in the organisation

Average annual sales: The average annual sales per person prior to the investment

ROI: The return on the investment

Using the same example organisation as in the Productivity part of the formula, and taking $35,000 as the average salary, we would have the following:

$$100 \times 5\% \times \$520,000 = \$2,600,000$$

So, with the above example, with each person showing an average 5% increase in sales of $10,000 per week or $520,000 per year, the return is $2.6 million.

Obviously, this is the total turnover return and not the actual profit made. In this case, we would need to multiply the turnover by the profit. So, at 10% profit, the ROI would actually be: $260,000.

Don't forget, this is the net gain. The ROI still has to go through the original formula which is:

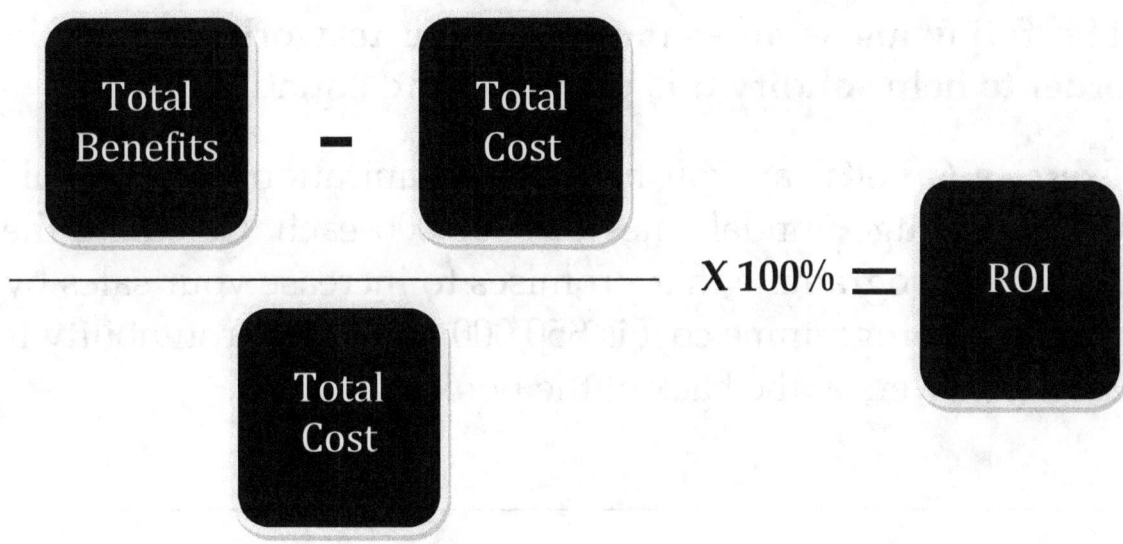

As we have no cost of the programme illustrated here, we will suggest it cost $40,000 to implement. The ROI therefore would be:

($260,000 - $40,000) / $40,000 x 100% = 550% ROI

The following is an example for you to work through in order to help solidify this principle and equation:

Exercise 6. Let's say you have an organisation of 50 people taking average annual sales of $350,000 each. Calculate the ROI on a programme that promises to increase your sales by 10% if the programme cost is $50,000 and your profitability is 20%. (Answers at the back of the book.)

_____

_____

_____

_____

As an interesting point in business, when you are increasing sales without increasing overheads very much, the net profit becomes a lot closer to the gross profit. So, this 10% may be closer to 30 or even 40%!! This is due to the fact that the set overheads are already taken care of such as rent, power, salaries, etc and the additional income adds little or nothing to the existing overheads.

As a final comment, costs of programmes won't just be the money you hand over to the training provider for example, it will also include the downtime for that staff member attending and this should be taken into account. The purpose of this formula is to keep things as simple as possible. If the ROI looks like a close call, you may need to look at it in more detail or you may consider some of the softer measures explained previously as they will tip the scales.

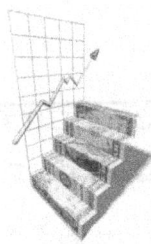

Chapter Eight - RPMs Methodology

Although the RPMs formula can be applied to many things, it is the methodology which provides the flexibility and concept to give the results required for justification of expenditure. The methodology is defined as: 'The blending of hard and soft measures, the evaluation of the pinpointed expectations and accountability for the expenditure.'

This methodology can be used to determine the validity of expenditure and the justification of a business case. It is noteworthy to understand that the methodology can uncover a reason not to go ahead just as practically as a basis to start right away. The four phases shown here are:

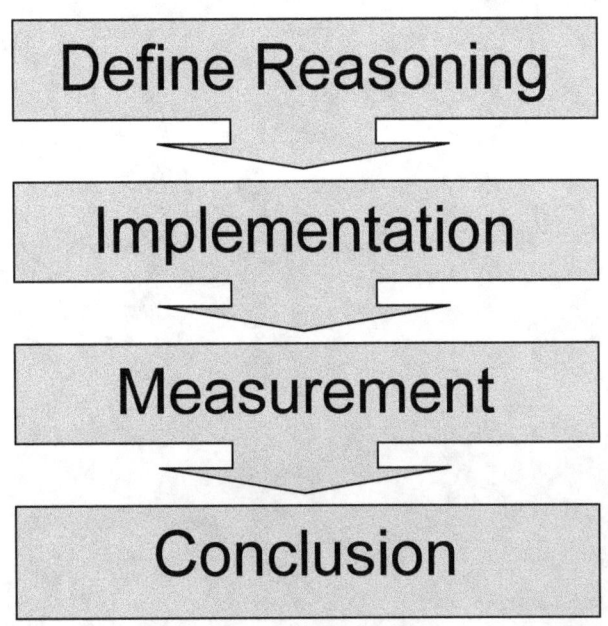

Phase One – Define Reasoning:

- Purpose of the business case
- Proposed action – summarise
- Business objectives
- Detail benefits
- Predict ROI
- Explain scenarios
- Threats & constraints
- Assumptions for success
- Sources of information

Phase Two - Implementation:

- Who will implement it
- Who will it affect
- Where will it be engaged
- What is required to implement it
- Time period for implementation

Phase Three - Measurement:

- Financial projections
- Cost savings projections
- Likelihood of results
- Before & after scenarios

Phase Four – Conclusion:

- Give additional options if available
- Make the recommendation
- Who's accountable
- Report on results

Phase One

The definition phase starts with defining the reason for the expenditure. If it's a training programme, reasoning might be to up skill the staff in sales techniques in order to maximise sales with every customer contact. Without the training, the company will continue to make the same amount of sales as before. If it is the purchase of a new computer, the reasoning might be to increase the capability of the operator by speeding up processes or allowing the use of software not compatible with existing hardware which will allow the company to perform other tasks and services to sell on to clients. In both these cases, the reasoning is clearly defined. Having a budget to spend is NOT a valid reason!

A summary of the proposed action should be clear and concise. This will alleviate any misunderstandings with others in the organisation, make it clear to the supplier (if any) what you are expecting to receive and even serve as a reminder to yourself should the initial project expand or be shelved for a period of time. As an example, ABC Company will be training our entire Customer Service team in a one day programme spread over three months. Or XYZ Company will supply new laptop computers to each sales person fitted with wireless internet connections and internet CRM licenses in order to update customer records remotely.

The business objectives should always be a consideration and in the event of extra weight being required to carry a project forward, the fact that it is clearly aligned with the business objectives will help immensely. For example, if the case is for a sales programme to enhance the skills of the team in order to close more business and the business objective is to increase revenue by 20% every year, then there is a clear match here with the purpose of the business case and the business objectives.

With clear reasoning or purpose of the business case or expenditure, you can now pinpoint the expectations of the expenditure. For the sales programme, that might be something like expecting revenue in the company to increase by 20% over the next six months. For the computer purchase, it may be something like the new software will be operating within the first week of installation and that at the end of that first week, the organisation can offer that service to the clients. In addition, the productivity of the operators will improve by a certain percentage due to the increased speed capacity of the machine. Expectations should be clearly defined so as to ensure everybody involved including the supplier of the goods or services is under no illusions that you're happy just to spend money!

There may be many benefits from the implementation of the expenditure. These should all be listed whether directly related to your business unit or heavily measurable. Just list everything. Example benefits of both our examples are listed here:

Sales Training Programme:

- Increased Revenue for the company
- Satisfied Customers due to the awareness of staff explaining better product or services benefits available
- Improved Morale of staff due to more skills and better results

New Computer:

- Increased productivity of staff
- More services to offer clients
- Bigger market to tackle with new services
- Increase revenues

Remember, as described earlier, listing benefits can be quite inventive and will include soft and hard measures. Everything should be listed down. Your list of benefits can be pages long. Then you should apply the 'So What' principle to each benefit. Drill down to see exactly what each benefit is likely to provide you with. Remember not to stop at the first line – keep going. In most cases you should be able to come up with a tangible benefit.

With any expenditure, measures will help determine if the expectations or promised benefits become evident. These measures should be defined up front and explained to all involved as part of the process to determine the success of the investment. Of course, some measures will be required prior to the start in order to make comparison. In the case of the sales programme, you will need to know what the current level of turnover is for the company and probably individuals' performance on a daily or weekly basis. For the computer, you may need to determine up front what numbers of tasks are normally performed in order to measure improved productivity. All of the measures should be straight forward and quantifiable – i.e., allow evidential change or hard figures.

With measures in place, an ROI prediction is then possible. This is where the RPMs formula can come in to play. By predicting a certain improvement in revenue or productivity by using the formulas described in the previous chapter, there will be some hard monetary expectations in place which may act as measures themselves.

The RPMs formula remember is:

Retention Gain + Productivity Gain + Morale Gain + Sales Gain = Total Gain

No. of people x (current attrition rate – target attrition rate) x $ cost to retrain = Retention Gain

No. of people x %increase in productivity x $average salary = Productivity Gain

No of people x Saved sick days per person per year x $cost of a sick day = Morale Gain

No. of people x %increase in sales x $average annual sales per person = Sales Gain

Predicting ROI

Ways to effectively predict ROI include:

- Use suppliers case studies. Have them come up with previous examples and references in the same area you are considering using
- Use the RPMs formulas to throw some figures in and see what is reasonable
- Use motivation surveys on staff to determine what they think will make a difference

- Talk to other people in the same industry who have tried programmes
- Run a pilot group or test period
- Use a control group

A powerful way to determine the benefits of either going ahead or making no change is to detail two scenarios. If you have spent some time analysing the measures available and come up with some figures of some kind, then there are two scenarios to examine:

Scenario One: What will happen if we go ahead?

Scenario Two: What will happen if we make no change?

You may be entirely convinced that going ahead with your proposed action is worthwhile, financially viable and indeed in the mathematical equation of things – a 'no brainer', you should ensure that you have covered all of the angles. The last thing you want is to make a presentation to the board or your colleagues, business partner or whoever and be very excited only to discover that someone asks you a question that could implode the whole case. To ensure well balanced presentation, look at what may impact on the implementation. This can be covered in the Threats and Constraints category. This will include things such as costs to implement, people away from their roles to be trained, the knock on effect of a huge influx of sales (a nice problem to have, although not much good if all you succeed in doing is annoying customers by not being able to process their orders or provide terrible service).

It is worth taking some time up front to analyse these effects as it may just prove to be too much difficulty to implement. However, if you have done the pre work on these areas, it shows you have thought ahead, covered the downsides and provided a solution.

There may also be other factors to consider. One of the biggest 'out clauses' going will be when a supplier will say, "Well, we didn't count on that happening" or "How could we tell a war was going to break out 10000 miles away?". These types of impacts on success can be covered off in advance. For example, an assumption for success may be that current market conditions dictate a requirement for your product or that so long as there is no change in the board of directors for a set period of time. It may not be possible to cover all eventualities but some forethought may help to show that some things outside of your control may still make an impact on the success of the programme or the investment.

As back-up to all of this information such as sales predictions, impacts on business, provide details of the sources of information. This will include things like:

- Supplier business plans
- Guarantees from suppliers
- Case histories from those who have implemented your recommendation before
- Survey results from staff
- Anything that shows support for your case

In all these cases, if you are using an external supplier – ask them for everything they have. If they cannot support you with the relevant information and are not willing to give you a guarantee of sorts, FIND ANOTHER SUPPLIER!!

Phase Two

Implementing the expenditure or making the investment is the fun bit. This is where you actually get to spend money. For those who hate spending money, this is the part where you take a deep breath and hope for the best. Going through Phase One should make this part a little less painful as there are some good reasons, measures and predictions already in place. If, of course, the predictions show a poor return or even a negative return, you can save your money and not go ahead. This is a lot cheaper than going ahead and then finding out you lost money!

Measures should be in place along the way where possible. These are much easier in a 'Roll out' or 'Pilot' scenario where the full investment is not made up front and you can determine the success of the programme before full commitment. It is essential that measures are in place early on. There really isn't a lot of point on measuring only at the end – it may be too late and besides, you will have spent the money.

With the data available from the measures, you can evaluate the performance. It's not much good gathering the information, then letting it sit somewhere. Evaluating is the process by which you use the measures to determine the success or failure of a programme. It also allows you the opportunity to make alterations. There is nothing wrong with altering a few things if it puts you back on track. If you can see it's not working out, somebody will thank you for saving money, time, effort or even tears should failure or little success be turned in to great success.

As part of the business case, there should be details of the actual logistics of the implementation. This is essential to show you have a route planned out with actual names and numbers attached.

If you belong to a large organisation, it is well to state who will be engaged in the programme or who will receive the equipment, etc. Don't assume everyone knows what you know.

In addition to who will be involved directly, detail who may be affected. Will extra staff be needed to be brought on board? Will the programme create extra work for another department? Will the power need to be turned off? Will new people be on site – do you need to let other departments know about anything?

There may be a number of sites in your organisation. Again, ensure there is no ambiguity here. Will it be in all sites or those named, etc?

At this point, also list what may be required to implement the investment. Will it be financial only or will people be required to work weekends; will the marketing department need to be involved?

Detail the time span. There should be a clearly defined schedule – this is massively important to allow for measures. Implementing a sales programme for example should carry with it an evaluation time period in order to measure its effectiveness. This all adds to the credibility of the project to show some accountability.

Phase Three

As mentioned in the previous phase, the measurement is extremely important. It will allow you to show proof for the investment (hopefully) and will certainly help to get sign off in times when budgets are cut or there is a downturn in economy – simply because you will have history to show how it worked in the past.

When trying to get sign off, you will be talking with those who are very analytical – these are often accountants, directors or company boards. In any case, whether you are left brain oriented (analytical) or right brain (creative), you will do well to convert the benefits into something tangible to illustrate the equivalent monetary gain or value.

Financial projections are going to be the carrot for most business case successes. Here you should detail the projected benefit in monetary value to the organisation. This is an expansion of the predicted ROI showing actual net gain in dollar value to the organisation.

 As an example, a programme which predicts an increase in sales of 20% when your turnover is $20 million will give you another $4 million in turnover. A profitability factor of 20% will then give you a net gain of $800k (less the programme implementation costs). If the programme implementation costs were $100k and the increases were projected for one year, it's a pretty strong

case. It effectively states that for $100k today, you will return $800k throughout the year!!!

It may be that your case is built around saving money as opposed to making more (which amounts to the same thing – bottom line profit). It just may mean you putting the financial benefits in a slightly different light. For example, if you know that by implementing a rewards programme for your staff, you know that you reduce the attrition rate from 30% down to 15% you can determine the saving on retraining costs. Using the formula from the example earlier on in the book where 100 people and a retraining cost of $15,000, you would be showing a cost saving projection of (100x15%x$15,000) = $225,000 – or to put it another way, every year you don't go ahead it's costing $225,000!

In this measurement phase, add in some comment on which assumptions made earlier for success will make the biggest impact. As an example, if one of the assumptions you made was that the ROI would be solid so long as your product was still required in the market place over the next 12 months and then suddenly your product was linked to a series of confirmed mishaps with the public; no matter how good the sales programme was, public opinion may cause a giant boycott of your product which does not mean the sales programme was unsuccessful.

You can add further weight to your case if you can highlight the likelihood of results.

For example, try to predict a percentage probability of breaking even or of meeting 50% of target or even 200% above target. This will show some additional angles for people who fixate on the target alone. Firstly, let's say that even if you don't get to target but to break even is 95% likely – that may be enough of a sure bet for most people to give it a shot. Secondly, if your likelihood of 200% above target is also a possibility, it shows that an extra bonus is possible. Sometimes people talk in language relative to a payback period. Energy efficient lamps are a good example. This is when you pay more for the lamps themselves but they consume less energy and last longer than regular incandescent lamps. Over a period of months, the savings on energy consumption and replacement costs becomes even with – and then less than – continuing to use the regular lamps.

Finally, illustrate the before and after effects. We've all seen the photographs of some beauty treatment and thought, "Well, if it's that good, I'll take it!" It can be very powerful to show what you could have compared to what you have now. This can be shown financially, graphically or pictorially. It should be a summing up of the measurement phase.

Phase Four

In a later chapter, we will discuss the topic of accountability in more detail. Here, it is the crowning point of the process. This is the reporting stage. Rolling out a programme of investment in training, IT expense, marketing or anything else means that a number of people are affected and helping along the way and they deserve feedback. Reporting should go both ways – up the line and down the line. If you had just won the jackpot, you would want to tell everyone! If you had a successful programme, you probably would too. If things didn't quite go according to plan, you may feel like burying the results. If you made the decision, the accountability lies with you and it should be shared with others involved in the process. So much can be gained from that reporting. Failures will happen and errors will occur. Sometimes results are the error themselves and are never corrected because someone doesn't report on them.

In the conclusion phase, also list other options considered. Here you may have to give information you may not like to give. Very often there will be a middle option which is not as good or not as easy for you. However, if you have thought of enough benefits to go ahead with your option of choice, you will also have enough reasons over and above the middle option. Again, showing other options will show you have explored more than one angle.

As well as explaining who is accountable (probably you), the recommendation should be made. Do not leave this part out as it is like asking for the business in a sales presentation. You can do everything right and then wreck it at the end by not concluding with the recommendation. This shows that you are putting your name to the case.

The final part is to report on the results. You may have had a number of people assist with the recommendation and putting together the business case. It is at least common courtesy to inform them of the results. If you've done everything right, you will probably be shouting it from the roof tops anyway because you will get the results. It's just one of those things that a lot of people don't measure and therefore have no idea what their investment got them.

The applications of this methodology can be manifold and examples of such are presented in the next chapter.

Chapter Nine - Applications and Examples

When you start thinking about it, there are seemingly limitless applications for the use of this methodology and these formulas. It really doesn't matter what line of work you are in, the possibilities for justifying expenditure or not can all be worked out. Over the next few pages, we will investigate three example areas: HR Initiatives & Training, Marketing and Capital Expenditure.

HR Initiatives & Training

The practical measurement for these programmes is often too difficult to measure. In so many cases sign-off just isn't given because positive business impact just cannot be achieved. Well, that is until this methodology is applied and the RPMs formulas are integrated with the business case. A perfect example of this was with a large New Zealand retailer with a finance call centre. The Call Centre Manager requested a number of times for a wellness programme to be instigated but each time, the plan was knocked back. The same plan was put forward with the use of these formulas illustrating the monetary impact it could have on the business due to the morale and health of the staff being improved. Sign off was given immediately.

A survey carried out in New Zealand by Deloitte Human Capital and The Learning Curve and published in the October 2003 Management Magazine highlighted that less than 20% of organisations that were surveyed measured any tangible business impact in their HR programmes. In the same survey, it was found that 42% of businesses don't monitor the cost of absenteeism and employee turnover!

As a company, one of the simplest questions we would always ask of our clients was, 'What is going to tell you this programme has been successful?' A number of organisations couldn't answer. To us, it was fundamental that there should be some way of telling, or some measure that identified, the desired result. Basic in its offering, this question alone changed the way people viewed training. It wasn't a budget filler – it could actually provide some benefit to the business. If you are currently using providers for HR initiatives, ask them what your ROI will be for your investment. If you don't know what the 'R' (Return) is, then the 'I' (Investment) is always a 'C' (Cost).

One of the common reasons people choose not to proceed with a training programme or other HR based initiative is that there is a downturn in the economy. In defining what happens in a downturn, there is basically a potential drop in available business or custom. However, the number of competitors in that market tends to remain constant.

Therefore, a downturn is the time when HR spending should increase in order that your staff members are more skilled and able to win, secure and keep the 'less amount' of business that is out there.

Marketing

How valuable is marketing in your organisation? I bet there's some sort of budget for it or that somebody thinks there should be. Think about all the places you eat at, all the clothes you wear, the products you buy. You are bombarded with marketing to help you decide to buy a certain brand.

Unless you have recently arrived from another planet, you will recognise a number of leading brands just by their logos or even colours. It has cost companies a huge amount of money to get their branding recognised in worldwide markets. Brand recognition is measurable through surveys and should be measured in that way at least to determine if the marketing campaign is working. The surveys should also be directed at the target market. There isn't much point aiming marketing of some young and trendy product to the retirement age community and secondly not much point surveying members of that community if they recognise the brand – it must be the right kind of measure.

In marketing, certain measures can be extremely effective. For example, the number of leads from a campaign can be measured to determine its effectiveness. It will also help if the front line sales staff are consulted before a campaign is launched. So often, the marketing department miss out on valuable and easy access information on those who are interacting directly with the target audience simply by not entering into communication.

Capital Expenditure

One of the great benefits of this type of investment over HR initiatives and Marketing is that you actually get something tangible with the expenditure. You may have a brand new photocopier sitting in the office or a new computer on the desk or some telephone asking you what time you want your morning snack. So very often, this type of expenditure wins over other budgets because it's a physical asset. It is true that the visibility of the investment is a justifier in itself. However, in listing assets, the greatest assets should be considered to be the right people in the organisation.

A capital expenditure should also have the same reasoning as any other investment. A new machine for example could be requested by factory staff to aid in the process for manufacturing widgets. Let's say the old machine breaks down once a day losing an hour's production. A new machine may cost $40,000 as a capital investment. An hour out of the 24 hour shift running represents 1/24 of lost productivity each day. It also means that for 1/24 of the day, the wages are being wasted by those involved in that process at least. If the production lost per day equated to $120 of lost product being made and $50 of labour time lost, a 365 day operation would see $62,050 saved each year by purchasing the new machine. There may be a number of other factors to put in the equation but in a simplistic view, it already shows that the machine could be paid for in less than eight months and for the next few years; the organisation will be saving the $62,050 each year as well.

There are many other examples that can be cited for applications of this methodology. ROI is not a new topic but providing a simplistic methodology with proven formulas is something many organisations are looking for. The RPMs Methodology is a proven way of providing a hard measurable return on sometimes previously regarded soft measures.

Recruitment

One of the most common areas of concern is for businesses to take on extra staff members and can they afford to. Well, this should be pretty simple really. By applying this principle, you should be able to determine very quickly whether or not it is worth taking on the extra staff member, opening up the new area, splitting a department etc, etc. Here are a couple of examples:

1. Adding a Sales person to the team:

To condense the phases here, we know the reason is to increase sales. We must list the costs of taking on the new salesperson. These will be salary, car, insurances, recruitment costs, other benefits etc. Let's say these all amounted to $80,000. So long as you are measuring other areas of your business like turnover and profitability you should be able to discover the requirement to create a positive ROI. Let's say the profitability on sales is 25%, we can work out that: $80,000 / 25% = $320,000. This means that so long as you are looking for a payback or break even in year one, the sales person needs to bring in an additional $320,000 worth of business.

If your organisation is turning over $2 million with two sales people and your market share allows it (i.e., is small enough to allow the increase) then it would seem that $320,000 is a fairly easy target (of course there are lots of other factors to consider such as sales person's ability, length of tenure of existing sales people etc).

If you were looking for a payback within two years, then just adjust the total costs for the sales person over two years which may be $145,000. $145,000/25% = $580,000. So here, so long as the new person brings in above $580,000 over the next two years, you have achieved a positive ROI. To ensure you are getting a good ROI, you may set as a target $500,000 a year. This will provide a profit of $250,000 less the expenses of the sales person of $145,000 = net gain of $105,000 over two years or an ROI of 72%.

2. Taking on board an admin person

 Let's say a small businessman is considering taking on board an admin person to relieve him of some time. He's not sure whether he can afford to take them on board. Analysing his time, he finds he will save 30% time and pay the person $25,000 to work part of the week. His extra time can be spent doing what he does best which is to secure more business. Of the rest of his time, let's say only 50% was spent originally selling which means that now he has another 60% effective extra selling time (30% / 50% x 100% = 60%).

If the businessman currently turns over $350,000 for the business with a profitability of 35%, he is effectively giving himself the opportunity to increase turnover by 60% to $560,000 or by another $210,000 and with a profitability of 35% that's $73,500 in profit. The admin person was going to cost $25,000, so that's a net gain of $48,500 or an ROI of 194%.

Chapter Ten - When to Say No

A good salesperson knows when to walk away from a bad deal. Sometimes, the figures will just not stack up. This is the same view you should take when calculating the ROI on any investment. The whole purpose of keeping the methodology and the RPMs formulas simple is to give a straight forward view on whether something will be worth investing in or not.

In basic terms, if your return is going to be less than the investment after all the benefits are identified, it's time to walk away or say no to the investment. Remember though, that the benefits may be available for years after the investment. An annual saving of about the same cost as the investment for year one may provide greater sums in profit to the organisation in years two and three and so on. It is critical that the list of benefits incorporate timings as well as measurable advantages.

What's the point in taking weeks, involving a number of staff in doing a detailed analysis in something which will only provide a small ROI? The chances are that you will have lost the benefit in the time and resources tied up in getting the resultant figures in the first place, then you'll have to go ahead just to try and break even.

Using the simplistic methodology will still give you a relatively high accuracy and can be achieved in minutes normally.

 As a manager, you may want to use the 'So What?' technique explained in an earlier chapter when dealing with your staff. If they cannot justify the investment, there's a lesson right there in two words.

So what's a reasonable ROI? We have been asked this on occasion and it's really one to be reflected on from case to case. Certainly a 1% ROI is still positive, although may not be worth the hassle. A business case showing something in the 10,000% ROI also is likely to put people off. It has the connotation attached that says, 'Someone's made a mistake somewhere – it's just too high.'

Certainly, it's a question for people to consider on their cases but as a rule, we have found that anything from 50% to 500% is a good indicator of a worthwhile course of action, so long as the figures are accurate and supportable. Remember, someone should be accountable as we discuss in the next chapter.

Chapter Eleven – Accountability, Mankind's Vanishing Virtue

Responsibility for our actions is something we are taught at an early age. In our personal lives however, that level of responsibility for own lives takes a different route when we become adults. It is true that while growing up we are often accountable to our parents or guardians but as mature adults, we probably experience accountability at work in some respects – especially in regards to our time for wages exchange but are not all that familiar with 'personal life' accountability.

In some ways, this culture may reflect on our working life too. For example:

1. Are we accountable to our customers by showing them how they are going to benefit from using the product or services we provide or are we just concerned about taking the money?
2. Are we accountable to the organisations by which we are employed by demonstrating how our ideas or expenditure will benefit the organisation rather than not caring to because it's not our money?

3. Are we accountable to ourselves by proving that what we are doing or going to do is actually going to have a positive and rewarding effect and outcome?

With great effect, the ROI concept applied to our time, effort and expenditures in all areas of our lives may alter some of the choices we make. Predicting an ROI and pinpointing expectations gives a sense of accountability, outcome and purpose.

 If someone asked you for $100 of your personal money, under what criteria would you give them the money? Think about that for a moment. Would you want some sort of guarantee that you were going to get it back? Would you like it back in the same state (i.e. currency viable?), would you need a receipt, would you want odds on a return?

The chances are, you would want some sort of indication on what you can expect in return at the very least. Well, what if it's your organisation's money – do you have a similar set of criteria to follow? Are you as thorough with your investments?

A representative from an organisation that attended one of our ROI workshops stated that they had just spent a substantial amount of money on some management training and had no idea what they got for their money. Whose fault is that?

Are you burning your money? Would you give your $100 to watch someone else burn it? Probably not. Yet in some ways, this is happening in the business world everyday. If we cannot measure what we get for our money or our investment, we might as well just burn our money. Now you may think that you must be getting something for it – definitely more than just burning the money. Well, what? What do you have without measurement? You certainly will find it difficult to get sign off for a business case again of you have no idea what impact your last expenditure had on the business – especially if you have no measures.

Starting right at the beginning, you must have the reason first and then an idea of what will tell you it's been successful. Then you can put some measures in place and engage in the process.

As we discussed in an earlier chapter, there needs to be some accountability in place in order for the case to work. If you are putting the case together, then it is likely that you will have to put your name to it. If you require additional help and you are using an external supplier, then ask help from them. Any supplier worth their hire should be able to back up their plans, product, service, recommendations. If they can't, then how on earth do they expect you to believe them? Likewise, how can you expect sign off for a project if you have no supporting material or you aren't prepared to put your name to it?

Ownership, accountability and responsibility are all words that are often used but seldom evident in business. Take hold of the opportunity in doing a business case and in the outcome. Nothing will sell a case more than by endorsing it with your name as the one who will be responsible for the success of the project.

Chapter Twelve - Ten Tips for getting a business case signed off

1. Define clearly the reasoning behind the investment.

2. Pinpoint your expectations of the investment.

3. Ask your supplier or service provider to provide you with an ROI.

4. Predict the ROI.

5. Measure everything you can or at least estimate it. Count every available benefit:

   - Immediate Financial Benefits
   - Alignment to business objectives
   - Soft measures which may have no measurable component such as improved teamwork or freeing up spare time

6. Apply the RPMs Methodology and formulas to indicate monetary impact for the business.

7. Illustrate what measures will be in place during the roll out to monitor the progress and expectations.

8. Put a reporting procedure in place to show that there will be accountability for the project.

9. Get buy-in from the staff members and secure their ownership.

10. In the business case, illustrate how much it will be costing the organisation not to go ahead.

Answers to exercises

Page	Exercise	Answer
23	1	100%
33	2	150%
57	3	400%
61	4	200%
65	5	300%
70	6	600%

Recommended Reading List

The following is a list of recommended books that will assist you in your day to day running of your business.

Accountability in Human Resource Management
  – Jack Phillips

Costing Human Resources – Wayne F. Cascio

First Things First – Stephen Covey

7 Habits of Highly Effective People – Stephen Covey

The E-Myth revisited - Michael Gerber

The One Minute Manager – Spencer Johnson

Who moved my cheese – Dr Spencer Johnson

"Calculating the ROI added weight to a project that many GM's would often regard as non-business critical. Without a doubt using the ROI formula enabled us to justify expenditure for a team wellness program by showing the long term cost savings! Rapid Result's ROI formula should be in every manager's toolbox!"

"Rapid Results encouraged us to take a snapshot measure of our business before the training and after so we could calculate the return on the training investment. What we discovered was that we obtained an 55% increase in our service bookings, 65% increase in our vehicle testing bookings and 100% increase in our sales leads in **one month** which equated to an ROI of **160%** in the first month alone!!"

"The information really got me thinking on what I can do to justify my business case."

"A thoroughly enjoyable workshop - excellent presentation and extremely applicable information which I can use right away."

"Clarified the way to measure some softer skills & behaviours."

"I gained tools to look at benefits in a more tangible form."

"Practical workings to apply to current and future projects."

Derek Good Bio

Derek is an author, actor, presenter, facilitator, voice over artist, husband, father of four children and currently a director of LearningPlanet Limited which helps improve the productivity of organisations and the confidence of their staff through sales, service and leadership skills in bite-sized videos and short training modules.

Derek is a facilitator who works with leadership teams in LEGO Serious Play, TMI profiling, problem solving and strategy sessions.

He was previously the Managing Director of Rapid Results - a leading New Zealand training and consultancy firm specialising in contact centres. There he was responsible for spearheading customer relationships programmes and managed all the sales and communications functions for the business.

Derek has over twenty years' experience in general management in the UK and New Zealand market, is an Author of several books on leadership, coaching, sales, Return on investment, training activities and humour. He has also been a past winner in the Westpac Enterprise Auckland North Shore Business Excellence Awards and the TUANZ innovation award for Education.